A GARDEN OF EMOTIONS

Cultivating Peace
through EFT Tapping

with 10
instant videos by
Brad Yates

Illustrated by
Deborah O'Connor

At Eifrig Publishing, our motto is our mission —
"Good for our kids, good for our Earth, and good for our communities."
We are passionate about helping kids develop into caring, creative, thoughtful individuals who possess positive self-images, celebrate differences, and practice inclusion. Our books promote social and environmental consciousness and empower children as they grow in their communities.
www.eifrigpublishing.com

© 2018 Brad Yates

Printed in the United States of America

Published by Eifrig Publishing,
PO Box 66, Lemont, PA 16851, USA
Knobelsdorffstr. 44, 14059 Berlin, Germany.

For information regarding permission, write to:
Rights and Permissions Department,
Eifrig Publishing,
PO Box 66, Lemont, PA 16851, USA.
permissions@eifrigpublishing.com, +1-888-340-6543

Library of Congress Cataloging-in-Publication Data

  Yates, Brad
A Garden of Emotions: Cultivating Peace through EFT Tapping/
by Brad Yates, illustrated by Deborah O'Connor
p. cm.

Paperback: ISBN 978-1-63233-189-2
Hard cover: ISBN 978-1-63233-190-8
Ebook: ISBN 978-1-63233-191-5

[1. Emotions. 2. Self-Esteem. 3. Emotional Freedom Technique]

I. O'Connor, Deborah, Ill. 2. Title

22 21 20 19 2018

5 4 3 2 1

Printed on recycled PCW acid-free paper. ∞

Welcome to our Garden of Emotions!

Like in a flower garden, you can discover all kinds of beautiful things growing here in this garden of emotions: happiness, kindness, and excitement. But you might also find emotions you'd like to weed out, like anxiety, stress, fear, guilt, sadness, disappointment, or anger at yourself or others. Sometimes it is hard to enjoy the beauty of your garden with all the weeds in there, but they will crop up sometimes. And that is OK. You just need to know how to deal with them so they don't take over.

Our garden of emotions contains an array of videos that will help you get through all of these diverse emotions and learn to cultivate a feeling of peace, satisfaction, calm, positivity, kindness, and happiness inside. Tap along so you can enjoy all the good within you and share it with others!

You are a really great kid!

A GARDEN OF EMOTIONS

DMNGTMRYQL — Having a Good Day

Kindness to Self: Empathetic, Forgiving —

DPPCMFPYQX

DRZVMLDKTV

— Kindness to Others: Dealing with Shame, Bullying

Relaxing: Dealing with Anxiety, Stress —

DWMWJNSWSH

FKFNHDPGVR — Focussing: Getting the Wiggles Out

Letting go of Fear: Being Brave and Smart —

GQBTNQDZNP

GNLDFRNJBZ — Calming Down: Getting over Anger, Rage

Feeling Good Again: Getting over Sadness, Grief —

FYFBRFCNPB

GXCFDRHZXN — Being Positive: Dealing with Disappointment

Accepting Imperfection: Not feeling Good Enough —

HDCJYHYZNL

Scan the codes in with any QR barcode scanner on your smart phone! See back cover for details.

Foreword by Dr. Peta Stapleton

It is my absolute pleasure to have been asked to write this foreword to such a beautiful, practical, and much needed children's book.

As a researcher of the technique in this book for many decades now, I have witnessed first hand the positive effects it has on children's and teens' lives. Tapping (Emotional Freedom Technique) is a unique tool that is self-applied and reduces the feelings of stress and other distressing emotions very quickly. To be able to offer children and youth the ability to be in charge of their feelings, and have a way to change them, is very empowering.

Our research work has extended beyond clinical trials and led us to training teachers in tapping, to use it in a classroom on an everyday basis. As you may know, stress and anxiety levels amongst students and their teachers today are at an all time high. High stress levels have been linked to poor academic results in children, an increase in behavioral issues, as well as staff overwhelm.

Daily tapping practice gives children the opportunity to settle and calm themselves and develop focus. It may help them manage difficult thoughts and emotions. Tapping creates space, transforming impulsive reactions to thoughtful responses. Students may find it easier to get along with their peers and choose kindness and optimism.

It has been such a gift creating the program and watching the results unfold as teachers share tapping with children of all ages, and they then realise they have a way to choose different emotions.

A Garden of Emotions is a wonderful way to introduce tapping to younger children and assist them to truly cultivate peace in their lives. I hope you enjoy Brad's videos and tapping along.

Dr. Peta Stapleton is Associate Professor, a registered Clinical and Health Psychologist, Australia's leading researcher in EFT (Tapping), and based at Bond University on the Gold Coast. Peta is the developer of *Tapping in the Classroom, Evidence Based EFT for Health Professionals,* and a Certified EFT Trainer for EFT Universe. She is the author of *EFT For Teens* (2017) and *EFT for Introverts* (2018).

An Introduction to Tapping with Children
by Brad Yates

It almost goes without saying that tapping is a great way to help kids feel better when they experience uncomfortable emotions such as fear, sadness, and anger. Since so many of the issues that limit our health, wealth, and/or happiness today can be linked back to experiences that occurred in our childhood, tapping can also have a profound positive impact on the quality of their lives overall, enhancing their long-term joy and success.

Getting Yourself Clear

When deciding to tap with children, perhaps one of the best things you can do for them is to get clear yourself. If the intention is to "fix" the child, or clear something in them so that you can feel better, the effectiveness of the process may be limited. This is especially true if the child feels you are tapping with them because they are in trouble, and they may feel defensive. Ask yourself, "Why do I want to tap with this child?" See if any of the answers lead to a possible tapping round for yourself, such as:

"Even though I want to fix him …"

"Even though I'm hurting for her …"

"Even though these kids are driving me crazy …"

Get as clear as you can so that your intention is truly for the child's highest good.

Building Rapport

For many children, interacting with an adult can be intimidating – especially if the child is already in a compromised emotional state. While tapping can help ease this, it also helps to build rapport with the child first so that they are more willing to engage – and engage more fully – in the process. How to best build rapport will vary with different children, but some of the things you can do include:

- Getting down to their level so you see eye-to-eye.
- Using language with which they are comfortable – try to avoid words or concepts that go over their heads.
- Allow them to come to you, rather than forcing yourself into their space.
- Ask them to talk about what they are feeling – hear what their words are.
- Let them know that they are important.

Tapping with the Child

Once you have gotten clear yourself, and built rapport with the child, it's time to tap. To start with, identify the issue. As with adults, children could be bothered by a multitude of issues. If they are having trouble verbalizing what is upsetting them, some of the common things kids might tap on include:

- Feeling that a parent or teacher is mad at them
- Being angry at a sibling or friend
- Feeling like something is unfair
- Sad about something that has happened
- Not feeling well physically
- Fear about an upcoming event – fear that they won't do well

As with establishing rapport, you will want to use the child's words as much as possible. Verbally gauging a SUD (Subjective Level of Distress) level of 0-10 can be somewhat intangible for children. Therefore, it may be more effective to have them hold their hands together in front of them (representing a 0 – "not upset"), then spread them all the way apart (representing a 10 – "really really upset!") – then ask them to show you the level of their upset by how close together they put their hands.

How upset are you?

Not upset – 0   **Somewhat upset – 5**   **Very upset - 10**

In terms of a set-up phrase, use the words that feel most right for them. It may be as simple as: "Even though I'm sad…" or "Even though I have this yucky feeling…"
It may be more specific: "Even though I'm mad at Sophie for taking my doll…"
While many of us complete the set-up phrase with the statement, "I deeply and completely love and accept myself," this concept may, again, be a little intangible for kids. Some good alternatives may be, "I'm a great kid" or "I choose to feel good."

Before you start the tapping, if this is the child's first experience with tapping, tell them that you are going to show them a simple and fun way to help them feel better. Explain that there are "special" or "magic" points on the body (use your judgment on the wording depending on the age of the child), and that tapping on these points helps to clear away the bad feelings. (A description of tapping for kids is included at www.thewizardswish.com.)

As you tap through the various points, feel free to simply repeat the reminder phrase, i.e. "this sadness." If you feel comfortable, try other statements that you feel might be appropriate, such as, "this was unfair," "I'm still mad about this," and/or "it's not my fault." Take the child through a full round, and have them take a full breath. Have them rate how they feel again, and continue tapping as necessary.

Tapping in the Positive

It is helpful to also tap in the statement, "I'm a great kid." Too often, children get messages that can be damaging to their self-esteem. The tapping process offers a great opportunity to reaffirm positive statements that will have a variety of long-term benefits.

Positive statements can be included in the tapping round on clearing an uncomfortable feeling. Children can also be encouraged to do a tapping round – maybe daily – simply saying positive things about themselves, such as "I'm a great kid… I'm a good student… I'm kind and caring… I'm good at sports…" This works for adults, too. As a person taps while stating affirmations, the unconscious doubts are being cleared.

Tapping with Groups of Kids

If you are in a position to tap with a group of children, such as in a classroom, you have the opportunity to touch a number of lives in a positive way. In such a group setting, you may not be working with a particular situation, and may want to keep the tapping phrases more general. You might focus on tapping in positive statements, having the group tap along with you as you lead them to say, "I am a really great kid," "I am having a great day," and "I'm doing my best today." (The first video is designed just for this!)

It can also help to touch on the possible blocks that some of the children might be experiencing: "I might have some bad feelings… Maybe something happened earlier… And I'm feeling mad or sad… And I choose to let that go… I can let that go… I can choose to feel good…"

The tapping phrases might also be determined by what kind of group it is, and when the tapping is taking place. At the beginning of a class, you might have the children tap to feel focused, perhaps by tapping away the wiggles and giggles. Even tapping silently can help with this, as following your lead engages them in what you are doing, naturally leads them to focus on you, and will also naturally help them calm down.

Working with a group, you also have the opportunity to address some of the issues that you might find yourself tapping on with individuals, such as bullying or lying. Most if not all inappropriate behavior stems from low self-esteem. Tapping on these issues in a group provides a safe place to address these issues and how and why they are wrong — clearing defensiveness in the process — as well as cultivating the positive feelings that will minimize and eventually eliminate the need to act out in disrespectful ways.

The potential benefits extend outside the group tapping opportunity, as kids may well then tap with each other to help each other. Maybe they will also teach it to their families!

Conclusion

There are lots of possible benefits — both short-term and long-term — from teaching children to tap. Fortunately, children are also more in touch with their feelings, often making the tapping more effective. They are also less inhibited, and are likely to be more open to the process.

Disclaimer: While EFT has yielded impressive results in treating physical and psychological issues, not everyone will benefit in the same way. Brad Yates is not a doctor, and the information presented here is not intended to replace appropriate treatment by a physician or mental health professional. The instructions shown below can provide great benefit in feeling better, but are only a brief introduction to EFT. There have been no documented negative side effects from using EFT, and there should be no problem with your child doing the tapping as described here. However, different people require different care, and you must take responsibility for your child's well-being as well as your own. If you have any concerns, please consult a doctor prior to using this technique.

A Garden of Emotions:

Cultivating Peace through EFT Tapping

I choose to have a good day...

I choose to do my best today. The better I do, the better my day. And I can make it a really good day! I am allowing myself to feel really good so I can do and be my best today.

and I am a really great kid!

DPPCMFPYQX

I choose to be kind to myself...

Sometimes I don't think I deserve to be kind to myself.
But I choose to take good care of myself. And the bettter I feel,
the easier it is to be nice to myself and to others.

and I am a really great kid!

I choose to be kind to others...

Sometimes I am not nice to others and sometimes others aren't nice to me either. When someone is being a bully, they probably don't feel good inside. When I am nicer to others, I feel better and they feel better too. The more I can be kind, the more I can spread kindness. And the better I feel inside, the easier it is to be kind.

and I am a really great kid!

I choose to relax...

Sometimes I feel nervous, scared, or anxious.
Something inside me is telling me I need to be careful.
I can be careful, but I don't have to feel so bad inside.
I can relax and still make good choices. I am allowing
myself to breathe more easily and to calm down, and I am
taking really good care of myself while still being safe.

and I am a really great kid!

I choose to be more focussed...

Sometimes it is really hard to focus when you have the wiggles and giggles. But I choose to pay attention to what is important, because that is really good for me. I am letting go of my nervous energy so I can be right here, right now, and be relaxed and focussed.

and I am a really great kid!

FKFNHDPGVR

I choose to feel brave...

Sometimes I feel really scared and it doesn't feel good. What am I afraid of? I can be brave, but still be smart and not get hurt. Am I afraid of being embarrased? I don't have to feel bad because of what other people are thinking. I can let go of the fear and still choose to be smart in a brave way.

and I am a really great kid!

I choose to calm down...

Sometimes I get so angry or so upset. Part of me believes that I have a right to be angry and I need to be angry to get what I want. But I'd rather feel good and find solutions to my problems, so I choose to calm down. When I calm down, I think better, and I can think of the best way to get what I want.

and I am a really great kid!

I choose to feel good again...

Sometimes things happen that make me really sad, and that is good and that is normal. But I am ready to let myself feel good again now. I am giving myself permission to feel as good as I can. That doesn't mean I don't care about what made me sad, I am just ready to feel good again.

and I am a really great kid!

I choose to be positive...

Sometimes things do not turn out they way I want them to.
But I can choose to look for the positive in situations, in others,
and in myself. When I go looking for the best, I am more
likely to find it. Still some things don't go as I want and I don't
get what I want. That is disappointing and doesn't feel good.
It is not bad or wrong to feel disappointed, but I'd rather feel
better, so I am giving myself permission to feel better.

and I am a really great kid!

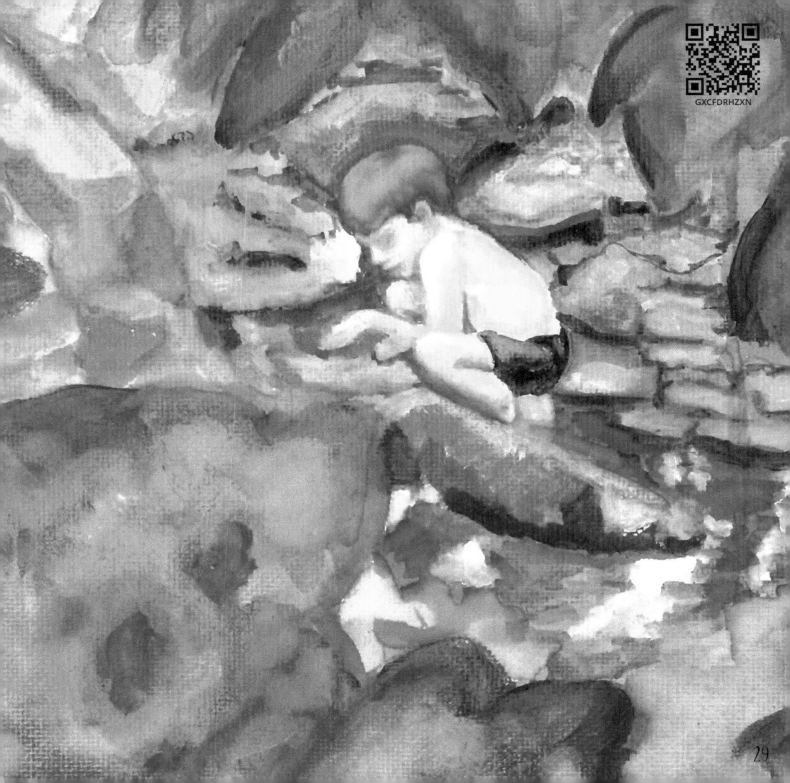

29

I choose to know I am good enough just the way I am...

Sometimes I feel like I am just not good enough. The more I remember that I am good enough, the better I do. And when I feel good enough, I can help others feel good enough, too. I am not perfect, but that does not mean I am not good enough. I have been good enough from the beginning and I am getting better all the time. And I choose to feel really good about myself.

and I am a really great kid!

About Brad Yates

Brad likes to think of himself as an Evolution Catalyst. He is known internationally for his creative and often humorous use of Emotional Freedom Techniques (EFT). He was trained and certified at the respected Hypnosis Motivation Institute in Tarzana, CA, where he served on staff. Combining this background with training in energy psychology and various schools of thought in the area of personal growth and achievement, he coaches groups and individuals in achieving greater success, health and happiness in their lives.

Brad has worked with a diverse group of clients, from CEO's to professional and NCAA athletes, from award-winning actors to clients in programs for homeless men and women and people in recovery from drugs. He has been a presenter at a number of events, including Jack Canfield's "Breakthrough to Success," several International Energy Psychology Conferences and the Walk On Water (WOW) Fest in Los Angeles. He is also the author of the best-selling children's book *The Wizard's Wish*, the co-author of the best-seller *Freedom at Your Fingertips*, and is a featured expert in the EFT movie *The Tapping Solution*. Brad has partnered on teleseminars with Joe Vitale and Bob Doyle of *The Secret* and has been heard internationally on a number of internet radio talk shows.

Brad has also performed internationally doing children's theatre, is a graduate of Ringling Bros. and Barnum & Bailey Clown College, and has two kids of his own.

www.tapwithbrad.com